Live Action

Jumping

Andrew Langley

Chrysalis Children's Books

First published in the UK in 2004 by
Chrysalis Children's Books
An imprint of Chrysalis Books Group PLC
The Chrysalis Building, Bramley Road, London W10 6SP

ISBN 1 84458 075 X

British Library Cataloguing in Publication Data for this book is available from the British Library.

Editorial Manager: Joyce Bentley
Project Editor: Clare Lewis

Produced by Bender Richardson White
Project Editor: Lionel Bender
Designer: Ben White
Production: Kim Richardson
Picture Researcher: Cathy Stastny

Printed in China

10 9 8 7 6 5 4 3 2 1

Words in **bold** can be found in Words to remember on page 31.

Picture credits and copyrights
Corbis: 1, 6 (Paul A. Souders), 10 (Mark Gamba), 11 (Ralph A. Clevenger), 19, 21, 23.
Digital Vision: 13, 15, 20, 24. Rex Features Ltd: 7 (Phanie Agency), 8 (James D. Morgan),
9 (Chris Martin Bahr), 12 (Action Press), 14 (Sunset), 17 (Ted Blackbrow), 22 (Henry T. Kaiser),
25 (Sipa), 27 (Reso), 29 (Lehtikuva). Steve Gorton: 4, 16, 18, 26, 28. Cover: Corbis/Larry
Williams (main image), Corbis (front inset centre right), Steve Gorton (back, front inset far
left), Digital Vision (front insets centre left, far right). Illustration page 5: Jim Robins.

Contents

Moving with muscles

You jump by pushing yourself up into the air with your legs. Both of your feet come off the ground.

People jump when they want to get higher in the air.

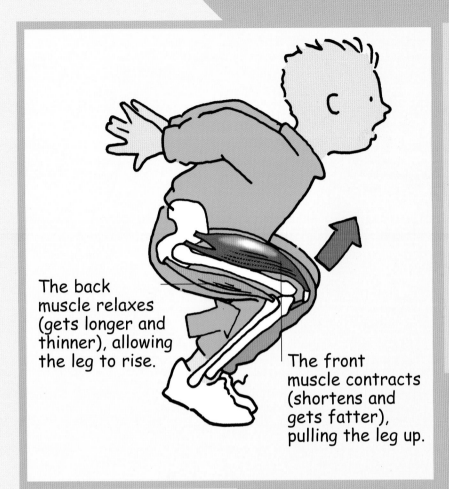

The back muscle relaxes (gets longer and thinner), allowing the leg to rise.

The front muscle contracts (shortens and gets fatter), pulling the leg up.

Muscles work in pairs. One muscle contracts while the other muscle relaxes. In this way, muscles move the bones in your skeleton forward to help you to jump.

About a third of a person's body weight is made up of muscles.

You use **muscles** to make you jump. Muscles move the bones of your legs at the **joints**, such as your hips, knees and ankles.

Crouching

To jump up you must crouch down. You bend your legs and then straighten them suddenly. This pushes you upwards.

A jumper hunches up her body ready to spring forward.

Lions crouch ready to jump on their **prey**. They bend all four legs to get as big a push as they can.

A lion keeps very low so that its prey will not see it.

Lions use their tails to help them keep balance when they jump.

High jump

To jump up as high as you can, throw your arms up. This will help you go up higher and keep your balance.

It is impossible to jump without bending your legs or ankles – try it!

Grasshoppers have six legs.
They use their two very strong back
legs to shoot them into the air.

Grasshoppers use
their powerful **leaps**
to escape from
predators.

Grasshoppers
can jump up to
a height of
more than
a metre.

Long jump

To leap a long way, you should take a run and then jump into the air. Your speed will help you to carry on going forwards.

Long jumpers throw their arms forward to help them jump as far as possible.

Frogs travel by jumping, using their powerful back legs. Their front legs help to steady them when they land.

A frog's back legs are much longer than its front legs. This helps it leap a greater distance.

Some frogs can jump more than 2 metres in a single leap.

over the top

You may need to jump to get over something that is in your way. Always look to see what is on the other side, in case it trips you up.

People run races in which they have to jump over special fences called **hurdles**.

A horse's hoof acts like a rubber pad to **absorb** the **jolt** of landing.

Horses are very good at jumping. They take off from their back legs and land on their front legs.

A horse can jump over fences up to 2 metres high and over ditches as wide as 6 metres.

Hopping

Have you ever played hopscotch? You **hop** on one leg, put both feet down, then hop again. You jump from square to square.

To hop on one leg at a time, your muscles have to work hard. Your legs will soon get tired.

The kangaroo hops along with its huge back feet together. At top speed, it can travel 12 metres in one hop.

A kangaroo can jump over obstacles almost 2 metres high.

A kangaroo uses its long muscular tail to keep it balanced as it hops.

Jumping off

If you jump off something, you will land on the floor. Let your knees bend a little when you land, to absorb some of the shock.

The higher the place you jump from, the harder your feet will hit the ground.

An eagle is a large, heavy bird. It can get into the air by jumping from a tree branch and spreading its wings.

When an eagle is about to land on a branch, it stretches out its clawed feet ready to hang on tight.

An eagle does not fall when it jumps off a branch. It flies using its big wings.

Jumping very high

If you want to jump really high, bounce on a trampoline. The trampoline's springs push you much higher in the air.

Hold your arms out to the side to help you balance as you jump.

A dolphin can be taught to jump through a hoop. It holds its fins out to the side to help it balance.

A dolphin can twist its body up and down and side to side.

Dolphins can jump high out of the water. They **flip** their tails hard to lift them into the air.

Jumping to reach

You can jump up high to reach a ball thrown into the air. You stretch out your arms and open your hands ready to catch it.

By jumping high, you can reach something at least one metre above your head.

Hens can jump up to peck berries off a branch or seeds from a food table. They help themselves get up higher by flapping their wings.

Large water birds, such as flamingos, can jump higher than humans.

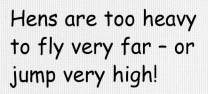

Hens are too heavy to fly very far – or jump very high!

Leaping in and out

When you jump on to something soft, such as sand or a mattress, its surface acts like a cushion that absorbs your weight.

Bend your legs to help soften your landing in the sand.

Salmon leap over small waterfalls on their way upriver.

Salmon swim from the sea up rivers to **breed**. With a flick of their bodies and tails, they leap high out of the water.

Brown bears wade into rivers to catch the salmon as the fish leap out of the water.

Jumping out

Do you want to give someone a surprise? When you see them coming, hide among the bushes. Then jump out suddenly.

Crouching down below other people's eye-level makes you more difficult to see.

A leopard is strong. It can climb a tree carrying a dead animal as heavy as itself.

A leopard tries to catch other animals by surprise. It hides behind bushes or long grass and springs out to grab its prey.

Leopards also hide in trees, looking out for prey. Then they jump down to attack.

Jumping for joy

Sometimes people like to jump up in the air or skip about just to show that they are happy.

Children jump for joy in a swimming pool. They make a big splash.

Young gazelle leap about in the dry grass. They are enjoying themselves but also learning to use the muscles in their legs.

Gazelles jumping for joy is known as 'pronking'.

Young gazelle have thin bodies and long thin legs. They can leap 2 metres into the air.

Landing

When you jump a long way, you can hold out your arms to help you keep balanced. This stops you from falling over as you land.

Curling up into a ball can stop you being hurt when you fall.

A giraffe has very long legs. When they are just born, baby giraffes find it hard to control their legs. Young giraffes sometimes fall over after they jump.

A baby giraffe can stand up about one hour after it is born.

The front legs of a fully grown giraffe can reach a length of 1.8 metres.

Facts and figures

The flea is the best animal at jumping.
Although it is tiny, it can jump up to 30 centimetres high.
If the flea was as big as us, it could jump 200 metres high in the air!

A kangaroo cannot jump at all if its tail is lifted off the ground.

The salmon can jump 4.5 metres out of the water.

A flying fish can jump out of the sea and glide through the air for about 100 metres.

Rabbits and frogs never walk. They always jump or hop.

The highest jump ever made by a human was 2.45 metres by athlete Javier Sotomayor, from Cuba, in 1993.

The longest jump ever made by a human was 8.95 metres by athlete Mike Powell of the USA in 1991.

The highest indoor skateboard jump is 5.5 metres and was reached by Danny Way of the USA in 2002.

A Russian scientist has invented a pair of jumping boots. Every time you put your feet down, pistons in the boots push them up again, shooting you into the air.

Words to remember

Absorb   To take, suck or soak up something so that it reduces in size or disappears.

Breed   To mate: males and females making eggs or babies.

Duck   To lower your head and neck to make yourself smaller so you do not bump into something above.

Flip   To flex or twist your body then straighten it.

Hop   To jump on one leg or on both legs together, usually moving forwards.

Hurdle   A barrier or obstacle to jump over, usually in a race.

Joint   A part of the skeleton where two bones meet.

Jolt   A sudden or quick hard knock.

Leap   To make a long jump forwards or into the air.

Muscle   A bundle of elastic-like fibres that can tighten or relax to move parts of our bodies.

Predator   An animal that hunts other animals for food.

Prey   An animal that is hunted and caught for food.

Index